Cornwall

Michael Bennie

COUNTRYSIDE BOOKS
NEWBURY BERKSHIRE

First published 2009
© Michael Bennie, 2009

COUNTRYSIDE BOOKS
3 Catherine Road
Newbury, Berkshire

To view our complete range of books,
please visit us at
www.countrysidebooks.co.uk

ISBN 978 1 84674 133 3

Maps and photographs by the author

Designed by Peter Davies, Nautilus Design
Produced through MRM Associates Ltd, Reading
Printed in Thailand

Contents

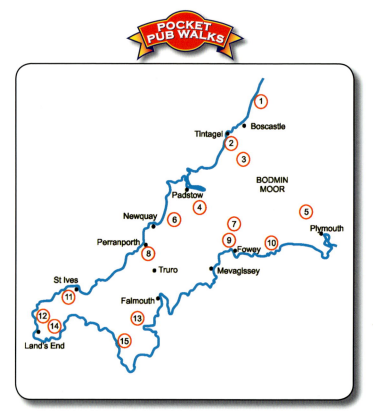

POCKET
PUB WALKS

1
Boscastle
Tintagel
2
3

BODMIN
MOOR
5
Padstow
4
Newquay
6
7
Plymouth
Perranporth
9
Fowey
10
8
Truro
Mevagissey
St Ives
11
Falmouth
12
13
14
15
Land's End

Area map showing location of the walks

Introduction

Cornwall has a wonderful variety of experiences to offer the walker. Although it is rightly renowned for its superb beaches, there is much more to the county than just sun and sand. From spectacular coastal cliffs to open moorland, from pretty woods to majestic rivers, from places of natural beauty to sites of historical and legendary interest, there is something for everyone.

In this collection I aim to introduce you to some of Cornwall's hidden gems – while not neglecting the more obvious attractions – and to a range of different landscapes and scenery. So although you will find many outstanding beach and cliff walks, there are also riverside paths, a route along the edge of Bodmin Moor, beautiful woodland ambles and an exploration of some fascinating places that give glimpses of the county's heritage.

In addition to its scenery, Cornwall also has some excellent pubs – and what better way to finish a walk than with a visit to a local hostelry to refresh oneself and reflect on what one has seen and done. Each walk therefore starts and finishes at an attractive pub – but of course, like the walks, the choice is based on my own preferences and impressions, and the descriptions reflect that. However, you will find a wide variety of establishments, their one common feature being that they offer a warm welcome to visitors.

Each entry comprises a description of the route and of the pub, and there is a sketch map for each, numbered to correspond to the numbered paragraphs in the text, but you may also like to refer to the relevant Ordnance Survey map; I therefore give the Explorer series map number and the grid reference. There is also information on where to park. Pub licensees usually have no objection to customers leaving their cars in their car parks while they walk, but some have very small parking areas – or none at all – and you may have to park elsewhere. Clearly, if you are not planning to visit the pub you should not use the pub car park anyway, and I suggest alternatives in each case. And even if you are planning to visit the pub, it is only polite to ask permission before leaving your car.

None of the routes covers particularly rough or boggy ground, although some cross short stretches that might become muddy after rain. Where this is the case I mention it in the introductory details, so that you can go suitably shod. However, stout shoes or light walking boots will be sufficient for every eventuality.

Finally, I would like to thank my son Jonathan and my friend Sarah Pym, who have provided accommodation and company during my researches, as well as my wife Katy, who has accompanied me on several of the walks and made some useful suggestions.

Michael Bennie

Publisher's Note

We hope that you obtain considerable enjoyment from this book; great care has been taken in its preparation. However, changes of landlord and actual closures are sadly not uncommon. Likewise, although at the time of publication all routes followed public rights of way or permitted paths, diversion orders can be made and permissions withdrawn.

We cannot, of course, be held responsible for such diversion orders and any inaccuracies in the text which result from these or any other changes to the routes nor any damage which might result from walkers trespassing on private property. We are anxious though that all details covering the walks are kept up to date and would therefore welcome information from readers which would be relevant to future editions.

The simple sketch maps that accompany the walks in this book are based on notes made by the author whilst checking out the routes on the ground. However, for the benefit of a proper map, we do recommend that you purchase the relevant Ordnance Survey sheet covering your walk. The Ordnance Survey maps are widely available, especially through booksellers and local newsagents.

POCKET PUB WALKS

1 Morwenstow

The Bush Inn

The coastal views on this route are quite stunning – at one point you can see the whole length of Bude Bay, as well as across to the island of Lundy. And the coast is very dramatic here, offering you a stimulating walk: rocky cliffs are punctuated by steep-sided valleys leading down to rock-strewn coves and beaches. As an added bonus, the hedgerows and path verges along the way are ablaze with wild flowers in the summer, and the silence is only broken by the sounds of the sea and the birds.

Cornwall

THE PUB The **Bush** is a 13th-century inn that was once the haunt of smugglers and wreckers. It now offers a warm welcome in its two bars, restaurant and extensive garden. The snug is a cosy little bar, furnished with settles, and with an open fireplace. The main bar is warmed by a wood-burning stove in winter, as is the restaurant. In summer, however, the place to be is the extensive garden, which has superb coastal views and a variety of children's play equipment. The food is almost all local – beef from their own farm, other meat from neighbouring farms, and local fish – and ranges from pasties, soup and ploughman's lunch to a variety of main courses, including local venison and pheasant.
Open from 11 am to 11 pm every day. ☎ *01288 331242*

1 Go back to the lane you came in on and turn left. After a few yards, as the lane swings right, go straight on along a track, following the sign to the **Coast Path**. Go through a gate and keep following the track on the other side. Go through another gate at the end and keep to the right of a field. You immediately get a fantastic view to the left around **Bude Bay**. Go through a kissing-gate at the end of the field and keep to the right again. At the end of that field you meet the **South West Coast Path**. You now get a good view to the right along the cliffs.

The view from the Coast Path

Cornwall

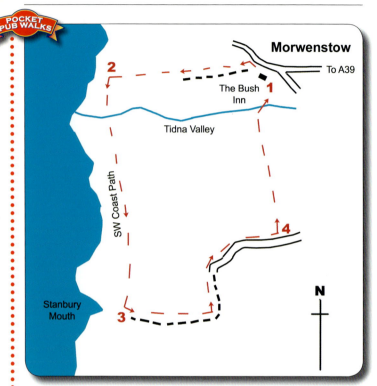

POCKET PUB WALKS

Morwenstow

To A39

The Bush Inn

1

2

Tidna Valley

SW Coast Path

4

Stanbury Mouth

3

N

2 Turn left along the **Coast Path**, and at the end of the field, follow it round to the right, and down as it descends steeply into the **Tidna Valley**, with occasional steps to help you. Cross a footbridge and climb some steps on the other side to a stile. Turn right on the other side and follow the path as it climbs. At the top, look right for another good view, with **Lundy** looming up out of the sea on the horizon behind you. The path swings left round a shelter, and you get another good view along the coast ahead. The path runs along an offshoot of the **Tidna Valley** and you cross a stile and climb. At the top, cross a stile and two footbridges. Go through a gap in a wall and through a kissing-gate. After a while you cross another footbridge and, shortly after that, go through a gap in another wall. The path swings right and then left, and descends steeply to **Stanbury Mouth**.

3 At the bottom is a T-junction; turn left to leave the **Coast Path** (marked as the footpath inland). Go through a gate onto a muddy track, which climbs steadily up the valley, with a stream bubbling down behind the bank on the right. When the track swings sharp left, follow it round, still climbing. At the top, go through a gate onto a lane and turn right. After 500 yards, you will see a farm on the right, with a gate immediately opposite. Just beyond the gate you will see a public footpath sign pointing across a stone stile to **Crosstown**.

4 Cross the stile and go through a gate on the other side. Bear right in the field beyond to a gate, a stile and another gate in quick succession. Go straight across the next field, with another good view to your left. At the end go through a gate and cross a track to another gate. Follow the path between walls to yet another gate. Cross the next field to a gate, and keep to the right of the next field. Halfway along you will find another gate, which takes you onto a path that goes down between banks and through another gate into the wooded **Tidna Valley**. At the T-junction just beyond the gate turn right and cross the stream. At the next T-junction, turn right (signposted to **Crosstown**). Climb some steps and go through a gate. Climb up the next field, go through one final gate and bear left. You are now in the garden of the **Bush Inn**.

Place of interest nearby

At Kilkhampton, about 5 miles away to the south-east, just off the A39, is **Brocklands Adventure Park**, with both indoor and outdoor activities, including a steam train, a soft play area and animals (☎ 01288 321920).

2 Tintagel

The Old Malthouse

Tintagel is steeped in history and legend. It is a pretty village, which is said to have been the home of King Arthur, and there is a great deal to explore, including the ruined castle on Tintagel Head. This relatively easy walk takes you through the farmland to the south, with superb views all around. It then drops down to join the South West Coast Path above the pretty beach at Trebarwith Strand. The return leg follows this path along the cliff-top to Tintagel Head and the castle, and back to the village.

THE PUB

The **Old Malthouse** is a 14th-century inn, full of character and atmosphere. It comprises three rooms. One first comes to the cosy bar, which has low beams and a wood-burning stove in an old fireplace at one end. Just off the bar is a light dining

> **Distance** – 3½ miles.
>
> **OS Explorer** 111 Bude, Boscastle & Tintagel. GR 055885.
>
> Apart from one steep climb in the middle, this is an easy route along clear, mainly flat paths and tracks.

Starting point The Old Malthouse. Customers may leave their cars in the pub car park while walking, provided they ask first. Otherwise there are several pay-and-display car parks in the village.

How to get there Tintagel is on the coast to the west of the A39 between Camelford and Wadebridge, and is clearly signposted from that road.

room, with its original stone fireplace and oven. And across a passage from the bar is the pretty lounge, which is furnished with comfortable armchairs, and which also has a wood-burning stove in an old stone fireplace. For fine days, there is a garden and outdoor seating. The menu ranges from soups, salads and sandwiches to steaks and, of course, a wide variety of fish dishes.

The pub is open all day most days, but the actual hours vary according to circumstances. It usually opens at 10 am, and being essentially a food pub closes at about 10 pm, when the last evening meal has been served. Hours may be a bit more restricted in winter, depending on demand, so it would be best to ring ahead if you are considering a winter walk, to warn them that you are coming.
☎ *01840 770461*

1 Turn left into **Fore Street**, and after a few yards right into a lane (signposted to the parish church and the **Glebe**). This takes you down into a dip and up the other side. When it swings right, go straight on up some steps and over a stone stile, following the public footpath sign. Follow the track on the other side to the right to reach another stone stile. Continue along the track on the other side and, when it peters out, go diagonally across the field to a stile halfway along the right-hand boundary. You now get a good view all around. Keep to the right of the next field, cross a stile and keep to the right of the next field. At the end, follow the hedge round to the left to a gate with a stile alongside. Cross to a track, which comes out at the end of a lane.

2 Cross straight over to another track, signposted to the **Coast Path** (do not go to the right, which is also signposted to the Coast Path). You now get an even better view, both to the left over a patchwork of fields and ahead along the coast. At the end of the track, go straight on to a stone stile. Bear left to another stile alongside a gate in the far left-hand corner of the field. Keep to the left of the next field to another stile, and keep to the left again. At the path junction about halfway along, go straight on to yet another stone stile. Turn right on the other side and follow

The Old Post Office, Tintagel

POCKET PUB WALKS

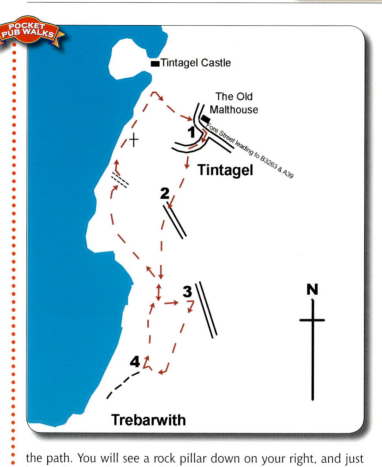

the path. You will see a rock pillar down on your right, and just beyond it a path going left. Follow it.

3 It comes out onto a lane; turn sharp right along a track (signposted to the **Coast Path**). You continue to enjoy superb views, both across the countryside to the left and ahead, and along the coast to the right. At the end of the track is a path between walls,

Cornwall

which leads down to **Trebarwith Strand**. At the path junction after about 200 yards, you can go straight on if you want to break the walk at **Trebarwith**, or turn right to follow the acorn waymark to continue the walk.

4 You climb some steps up to the cliff-top. It is a steep climb, but the views from the top are breathtaking. Continue along the **Coast Path** for about 600 yards and you will come to a short stretch of your outward route, passing the rock pillar down on your left. At the junction beyond it, however, you should go left, following the **Coast Path**. On the next section you will go through several gates and cross several stiles, but the path is quite clear at all times. After a while **Tintagel church** will come into view, and you will reach a track; turn left. When the track swings right, follow it round. It takes you past the church, and you will see the great bulk of **Tintagel Head**. You join a surfaced path and then go down some steps. At the bottom, go left if you want to explore **Tintagel Castle**, and right to return to the village. The path, goes down a hill and crosses a footbridge to a road. Turn right and immediately right again to join the footpath back to the village. It comes out onto **Fore Street**, and the **Old Malthouse** is on the left.

Places of interest nearby

There is a great deal of interest in Tintagel itself, including **Tintagel Castle**, which you pass along the route of this walk. This English Heritage property was built in the 13th century and was the home of the Earls of Cornwall. Although now in ruins, its situation on the edge of Tintagel Head makes it an interesting place to explore (☎ 01840 770328). In the village itself is the **Old Post Office**, a medieval farmhouse, one room of which was once used as a letter-receiving office (☎ 01840 770024).

3 **Blisland**

The Blisland Inn

This **varied route** combines open moorland with deserted lanes, flower-fringed in season (when I last walked it, in midsummer, the only traffic I met outside Blisland was one solitary horse rider). Leaving the village, which is clustered round its pretty green, it follows lanes and paths up to Trehudreth Downs, on the edge of Bodmin Moor, from where you can see across the whole district and beyond. After crossing the downs, more lanes bring you across Metherin Downs and back to Blisland.

Distance – 4½ miles.

OS Explorer 109 Bodmin Moor. GR 101733.

There is a steep hill on the way up to the downs, and one stretch of moorland is quite rough and boggy, so stout shoes or boots are recommended.

Starting point The Blisland Inn. There is no pub car park, but there is parking round the green opposite.

How to get there *The village is between the A30 just north of Bodmin and the B3266 Bodmin to Camelford road, and is signposted from both.*

THE PUB Set in an idyllic position opposite the village green, the friendly and atmospheric **Blisland Inn** comprises a pleasant bar with low beams decorated with beer mats and mugs, an attractive lounge similarly decorated and a family room at the back with a variety of games. The bar has a wood-burning stove and the lounge an open fireplace. There are also a number of tables on a patio overlooking the green. Bar snacks such as sandwiches (including their renowned crab sandwich) and baps are offered, as well as a wide range of main courses, including pasta and steaks.

Open from 11.30 am to 11 pm on Monday to Saturday and 12 noon to 10.30 pm on Sundays. ☎ *01208 850739*

1 Cross to the village green and aim for the far left-hand corner. Turn left along the road and follow it out of the village. As it swings to the right, you will see a wayside cross on the left, with a footpath alongside it. Take that and cross a stone stile. Bear right on the other side and cross the field to a gap in a bank. Keep to the right of the next field to a stone stile and some steps leading down to a lane.

2 Turn right and follow the lane downhill and across a stream. At the junction just beyond the stream turn left. This is a lovely stretch, with the trees forming an arch overhead and another stream tumbling down alongside you. Soon you turn left to cross the stream and pass the attractive old **Trehudreth Mill**. The lane climbs steadily between banks and trees for ½ mile and, at the top, it emerges into the open and bends to the right.

3 As it does so, go straight on through a gate onto the open moorland of **Trehudreth Downs**, and follow the track on the other side as it swings left. You get a superb view to the left

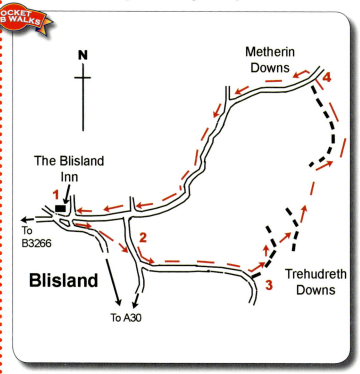

across the farmland, and to the right across **Bodmin Moor**. After ¼ mile the track goes left over a cattle grid; leave it to go straight on, following the line of the wall. You will find another track above you, which you will soon join. When this also swings left along the wall go straight on again, this time over open moorland, to meet up with a wall and fence about 200 yards further on. This stretch can be rough and sometimes boggy, but you should be able to find a way through or round the worst bits. When you reach the wall and fence the going becomes much easier, and you get a superb view to your right across the moor. When the wall and fence bend to the left again, go half-right, and as you come over the brow of the hill you will see another wall ahead of you. Aim for that, and when you come to it you will find a surfaced track running alongside it. Turn right and follow this track as it swings left to follow the line of the wall for ½ mile.

Trehudreth Mill, near Blisland

4 When the track meets a lane, turn left and follow it down to cross a stream, and then up across Metherin Downs. At the T-junction turn left (signposted to **Blisland** and **Metherin**). This is another lovely, tree-lined lane, which winds down past some pretty farmhouses for 2 miles back to **Blisland**. At the crossroads in the village, go straight on to return to the pub.

Places of interest nearby

Seven miles south of Blisland is **Bodmin**, where there are several places of interest, including the **Courtroom Experience**, where you can see a re-enactment of an old trial and decide for yourself whether the accused is guilty (☎ 01208 76616), the old **Bodmin Jail** (☎ 01208 76292) and the **Bodmin & Wenford steam railway** (☎ 0845 1259678).

4 St Issey

The Ring o' Bells

Two of Cornwall's long-distance trails are sampled on this interesting walk: the Saints' Way, which is based on an old route that links shrines and holy wells from Padstow to Fowey; and the Camel Trail, a disused railway that runs alongside the River Camel from Padstow to Bodmin. Farm paths take you to join the Saints' Way. You then follow it across fields to the neighbouring village of Little Petherick and on down through woods along the bank of the Little Petherick Creek to the outskirts of Padstow, where you join the Camel Trail. After a mile on this route, paths and lanes bring you back to St Issey. There are some excellent views, and both the creek and the river are full of bird life.

THE PUB The **Ring o' Bells** is an attractive old village pub. It comprises a beamed bar, decorated with old photographs, with a wood-burning stove at one end and a large fireplace at the other. Next door is a pretty restaurant with an old granite oven at one end, and outside there is a patio area. The imaginative menu ranges from pasties, baguettes and home-made soup to local fish and more exotic offerings such as jalapenos.

The pub is usually open from 12 noon to 3 pm and from 6 pm to 11 pm, although the evening session may start a bit later in the winter. ☎ *01841 540251*

1 Cross the A389 to a road and follow it as it bends to the left. Immediately after the turn, you will see a public footpath sign on the left, pointing right; turn right down a track. Go through a farmyard to a gate. You now get the first of the views – all the way to the wind turbines on **St Breock Downs** half-left.

Distance – 5¼ miles.

OS Explorer 106 Newquay & Padstow. GR 928718.

The paths and tracks are easily followed (although one stretch is rather muddy). There are a few climbs but none is too strenuous.

Starting point The Ring o' Bells. Customers may leave their cars in the car park while walking, provided they ask, and provided there are not too many vehicles in one group. If you are not visiting the pub, or there are a large number of cars, you can park in the pay-and-display car park at Little Petherick, and start at point 3.

***How to get there** St Issey is on the A389 between Wadebridge and Padstow. The pub is on the main road.*

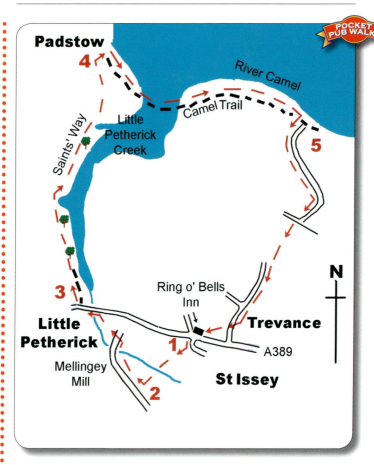

Bear right across a field to a gate and keep to the right of the next field to another. Keep to the right again down the field to a boardwalk and a footbridge and cross a stile on the other side. This is followed by some stepping stones and another stile. Bear right to yet another stile in the corner and go straight on along a drive past a house.

St Issey Walk 4

2 The drive comes out onto a lane; turn right. You are now on the **Saints' Way**. Follow the lane downhill, past the **Mellingey Mill craft centre**, and cross the stream at the bottom. The lane now climbs, and after about 100 yards you will see a sign for the **Saints' Way** pointing left. Follow it and climb some steps to a path, which leads to a stile. Keep to the bottom of the field on the other side, still following the **Saints' Way** waymark. Go through a gate at the end onto a concrete drive; bear right. Go through a gate at the end onto the A389 and turn left. Take care along here, as it is a busy road and there is no footpath. Follow the road for about 150 yards into **Little Petherick**, crossing the river.

3 Immediately on the other side, turn right towards the car park, following the public footpath sign with the **Saints' Way** waymark. Pass the car park and some houses, and follow the track on the other side. When the track goes left and begins to climb, turn right along a path alongside the **Little Petherick Creek**, still following the **Saints' Way** waymark. Climb into a wood, cross a stile and continue to climb, with steps to ease the way. The path skirts the top of the wood. At the end, cross a stile and keep to the left of the field on the other side. You now get an excellent view to the right, down the creek to the **River Camel**. When the wall on your left goes left, follow it round, and when you come to a gate on your left, turn right, following the **Saints' Way** waymark. The path skirts the field for a short distance and then goes left between high bushes. When you come out into the open, bear left and go down to cross a stile and a footbridge.

The path leads you over a muddy stretch to a boardwalk across the head of a side creek and up some steps. At the top you get another good view ahead to the **River Camel** and also to the right up the creek. The path runs along the right-hand edge of a field. Cross a stile at the end and keep to the right of the next field to another stile. Keep to the right again beyond that to another stile and turn left in the next field. At the end go straight on along the path between high bushes. Some steps take you down

The River Camel from the Saints' Way

to cross a footbridge and a stile; turn right on the other side. The path climbs across another field, with an obelisk erected to commemorate Queen Victoria's Jubilee over on the right. You now get a superb view up the creek to **St Breock Downs** again. Go through a gap in a bank at the top of the field and keep to the right. Cross a stile on the right at the end and turn left. As you go down the field, you get a good view across **Padstow** and the river. Go through a gate at the bottom and on down a track. After a few yards the track turns left and joins a lane; turn right.

4 After a few yards you leave the **Saints' Way**, turning right down another track, marked as the **Dennis Cove Lake Area**. At the end of the lake go left up some steps to the **Camel Trail**; turn right. After about ¼ mile the trail goes over an old railway bridge. After another mile, just after crossing a small creek, you will find some steps on the right, going down to a car park; turn down them.

5 At the bottom, turn right into a lane. After a short distance, you will pass the ruins of the **Halwyn Culver-house** on the right. 'Culver' is derived from the Old English word for a pigeon, and the house was therefore a large dovecote. The lane climbs, and after about ½ mile turns sharp right. After another 300 yards you will come to a T-junction; cross over to some farm buildings, following the public footpath sign. Pass them, and keep to the right of the field beyond to a gap in the hedge in the far right-hand corner. Cross a stone stile and then a wooden stile, and climb up the next field. As you go, look right for another good view across the **Little Petherick Creek** to **Padstow**. Go through a gate in the far right-hand corner onto a lane and turn left. At the junction after 250 yards go straight on to the hamlet of **Trevance**. Just beyond the 30 mph speed limit sign turn right along a track, following the public footpath sign. Continue round to the left and at the end go right along a grassy track to a gate. Follow the path round to the right to a stile and a gate, and cross the next field to another gate and another stile. Keep to the right of the next field, and at the end go left between some houses. You come out onto the A389; turn right to return to the pub.

Places of interest nearby

About 1½ miles south of St Issey is **Crealy Adventure Park**, a very popular theme park (☎ 0870 1163333). About 3 miles to the west, near Padstow, is **Prideaux Place**, an Elizabethan manor house, with extensive gardens (☎ 01841 532411).

5 Metherell

The Carpenter's Arms

Not only is this a beautiful walk, incorporating woodland stretches and river views, but there is a great deal of historical interest to see along the way – indeed much of the route passes through part of the Cornish Mining World Heritage Site. It crosses farmland to reach the National Trust's Cotehele estate, where woodland paths take you to a working mill and on to Cotehele Quay on the River Tamar, with the opportunity to visit the 16th-century Cotehele House and its gardens. You follow more woodland paths alongside the river and past mining remains before quiet lanes and farm paths take you back to Metherell.

THE PUB

The **Carpenter's Arms** derives its name from the fact that it was built in the 16th century to house workers involved in building Cotehele House, down the road. It has a cosy bar with a slate floor, a stone fireplace and dark beams, decorated

Distance – 3½ miles.

OS Explorer 108 Lower Tamar Valley & Plymouth. GR 409694.

There are several climbs, although none is too strenuous. One path towards the start is rather rough, but the others are quite easy.

Starting point The Carpenter's Arms. Customers may leave their cars in the pub car park while they walk, with permission. Otherwise the only parking is along the roads through the village. An alternative is to park at Cotehele Quay and start the walk at point 3.

How to get there *Metherell is about ¾ mile south of the A390 Callington to Tavistock road; turn off just west of Drakewalls.*

with ships' badges and furnished with settles and tables. There is also a large, airy restaurant. Outside is a patio with tables and an old well. The food is freshly cooked, and the bar menu ranges from soup and pasties to lasagne and other specials. There is a separate restaurant menu.

Open on Monday from 6 pm until they decide to close, on Tuesday to Friday from 12 noon to 2.30 pm and from 6 pm until they decide to close, on Saturday from 12 noon until they decide to close, and on Sunday from 12 noon to 10.30 pm. Food is not served on Monday, or on Sunday evening. ☎ *01579 351119*

1 Turn right as you leave the pub and, at the T-junction after a few yards, turn left. After ¼ mile, when the lane swings right, go straight on into a field. Follow the left-hand hedge and, when that turns left, go straight on across the field. You get a good view ahead, across the fields and woods. Cross a stile to a path alongside

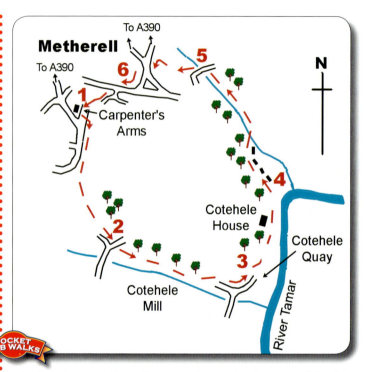

To A390

Metherell

To A390

6

1

Carpenter's
Arms

5

N

4

Cotehele
House

Cotehele
Quay

2

3

Cotehele
Mill

River Tamar

POCKET
PUB WALKS

a hedge. Cross another stile to a sunken path. This curves left after a while, and you come out onto a lane; turn left.

2 After about 200 yards you come to a T-junction. Go straight across to a gate. On the other side is a track leading into a beautiful cool wood; follow it for about 500 yards, where you will find a path going sharp right. If you want to visit **Cotehele Mill**, turn down here and cross the stream at the bottom. Non-members of the National Trust will need to pay at the office at the top of the path on the other side. In addition to the working mill, there are various workshops and outhouses with displays. If you do not want to visit the site, go straight on. At the end of the wood, go through

a gateway and straight on along the road on the other side. This leads to the **River Tamar** and **Cotehele Quay**.

3 The quay has an attractive collection of buildings, and also the restored Tamar sailing barge *Shamrock*. If you want to visit the house and gardens at this point, turn left up the drive here, following the signs. Otherwise cross to the car park and, at the entrance, bear left along a path into another pretty wood. The path climbs gently and you pass an old chapel. Shortly afterwards, you will come to a path on the left, leading up to the house and gardens (this route is open to National Trust members and ticket holders only – as indicated earlier, if you want to visit the house you should go up the drive from the quay). Continue along the path, and you will soon get a good view through the trees to your right, along the river to the impressive **Calstock Viaduct**.

4 You will come to some houses on the edge of the wood; turn left up a track, with a stream running alongside you on the right, and still with the lovely wood all around you. You pass a ruined outbuilding on your left, and a bit further on the old engine house of a disused mine, now a private residence, with the chimney still standing behind it. You cross the stream and pass another old mining building converted into a residence. The track narrows to a path, which is lined with wild flowers in season.

A view of the River Tamar from Cotehele Wood

Cornwall

5 You leave the wood and emerge into a lane; turn left. Cross the stream, and as the lane swings left go right. Do not follow the public footpath sign that points straight ahead, but turn immediately left along a track, following the sign pointing to 'the Mill'. Pass a house on the left and follow the path on the other side. It climbs into another wood. After about 300 yards it leaves the wood via a gate. Continue along the path that skirts the wood on the other side, with a meadow stretching down to the stream on your right, full of flowers for much of the year. At the end of the field, go through a kissing-gate into a lane and turn left. At the T-junction after 200 yards turn left (signposted to **Norris Green**, **Metherell** and **Cotehele**). After 100 yards there is another T-junction; turn right (signposted to **Metherell** and **Harrowbarrow**), and right again after another 100 yards (again signposted to **Metherell** and **Harrowbarrow**).

6 After another 300 yards turn left into a road called **Nicholas Meadow**. As it curves left, turn right down a smaller road. When that goes left, walk straight on to a kissing-gate and follow the path on the other side to another kissing-gate. Keep to the right of the field beyond to a stile; bear left along a track. When that swings right by some houses, go straight on through a gate onto another path, between a high wall and a bank. At the end cross a footbridge onto a lane; bear right and you will see the **Carpenter's Arms** on your right.

Place of interest nearby

Cotehele is well worth a visit. Built in the 15th and 16th centuries, the granite and slatestone house was the home of the Edgcumbe family, and the gardens are superb, stretching down to the wood and river below (☎ 01579 352711).

6 St Mawgan

The Falcon Inn

St Mawgan is an attractive little village, with an imposing 14th-century church, a craft shop, a village store and tea room, a pretty school and the Falcon Inn, all clustered together in the delightful, wooded Vale of Mawgan. And it is this valley that is the centrepiece of this walk. The route follows farm tracks above the left bank of the river and then crosses it and turns upstream along a path and then a lane. The last stretch is along another path back downstream through the beautiful mixed wood, alongside the river.

Cornwall

Distance – 4 miles.

OS Explorer 106 Newquay & Padstow. GR 873658.

The paths and tracks are very clear. There are one or two fairly steep climbs, but most of the route is relatively easy.

Starting point The Falcon Inn. There is a small pub car park, but while you are walking you are asked to park in the large, free public car park just behind it.

How to get there Turn north off the A3059 between St Columb Major and Newquay and follow the signs.

THE PUB The attractive 16th-century **Falcon Inn** is full of character. The long, beamed bar is furnished with pine tables and chairs, and has a large fireplace at one end. Beyond it is the slate-floored restaurant, and outside you will find a very pretty garden, with children's play equipment and a well. The food ranges from bar snacks such as pasties, jacket potatoes and burgers to local fish main courses, steaks and a daily 'specials' menu.

Open on Monday to Saturday from 11 am to 3 pm and 6 pm to 12 midnight, and on Sunday from 12 noon to 11.30 pm.
☎ *01637 860225*

1 Turn right from the pub and follow the road to the left, around the church. When it swings right again, go left up a hill. After about 150 yards you will see a gate on the right with a surfaced track on the other side. Go through and follow the track. You get a good view across the valley on the right. Soon you will find a wood on your right. When it ends, the track goes through a gate. Follow it along the edge of the field on the other side, with another good view, this time down the valley ahead of

you. Go through another gate and follow the edge of the next field. At the end is another gate, and on the other side the track passes some houses and becomes a lane. Follow it as it swings left then right around a small lake and climbs.

2 About ¼ mile after the start of the lane, you will find a track leading sharp right, marked as unsuitable for motor vehicles;

The lych-gate, St Mawgan-in-Pydar church

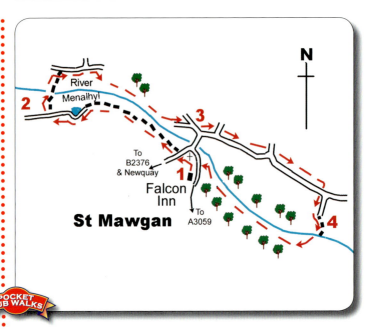

follow it down into the valley. At the bottom cross a footbridge and follow the track as it climbs up the other side of the valley. At the top you come to a lane; turn right. You pass a holiday park on your left, followed by a lane. Immediately opposite the lane, on the right-hand side, you will see a public footpath sign pointing through a gate. Follow the path on the other side between a wall on the left and a fence on the right to a stile leading into a small wood. In the middle of the wood you cross a stone stile. A bit further on you pass a house and go down some steps to a lane; go straight on.

3 After about 300 yards you come to a T-junction; turn right and then immediately left. The lane climbs and, after 150 yards, as it bends left, you should turn right down another lane. You continue to climb for about 600 yards to a T-junction; turn right (signposted to **St Columb**). After another 600 yards you come to another junction; turn right (signposted to **Higher Tolcarne**) and walk on to the end of the lane.

4 Bear right up a drive, following the public footpath sign for **Lawrey's Mill** and **St Mawgan**. When you come to a gate, bear left and after a few yards, at the next gate, left again along a track. This descends steeply into the pretty wood that stretches up from the valley. At the bottom cross a stile and turn left to cross a footbridge. Turn right on the other side along a path. After a few yards the path crosses a track; turn right and follow the track through the delightful wood, alongside the river. At the track junction, go straight on to climb above the river – although you soon meet up with it again. After about ¾ mile of this delightful woodland you come to the outskirts of **St Mawgan**. Turn right through a kissing-gate, following the signs, and you will come out at the public car park. Turn left to return to the pub.

Places of interest nearby

About 5 miles away is **Newquay**, with a variety of attractions, including **Newquay Zoo** (☎ 01637 873342) and the **Blue Reef Aquarium** (☎ 01637 878134). A similar distance in the other direction, at Winnards Perch on the A39, is the **Cornish Birds of Prey Centre**, with a variety of raptors and other birds, and flying displays (☎ 01637 880544).

The Ship Inn

This is a **delightful ramble** through the woods alongside the River Fowey and its tributaries. From the pretty riverside village of Lerryn, it follows lanes and farm paths, with good views through 180 degrees, to the beautiful Ethy Woods and the ruined St Winnow Mill. More farm paths take you to the hamlet of St Winnow itself and its medieval church, right on the edge of the River Fowey. The return leg runs through Ethy Woods again, first downstream along the Fowey and then up along its tributary, the Lerryn, back to the village.

The **Ship** is a characterful little 16th-century inn. Its small bar has low beams, a slate floor and a wood-burning stove. Beyond this is a light, airy restaurant, with a conservatory off it. At the back, there is a pretty beer garden. A good range of food is offered, from baguettes and ploughman's lunches to fish and chips, omelettes and grills.

Open from 10 am to midnight. ☎ *01208 872374*

1 Turn left as you leave the pub or the car park, and follow the road past the **Memorial Hall** and then round to the left to cross the **River Lerryn**. At the first junction, follow the main lane (signposted to **St Winnow** and **Lostwithiel**). At the next junction, turn left (marked as a no through road), and then, after a few yards, right along **Lerryn View**. At the end, turn right, following the public footpath sign. Go through a gate and cross the field on the other side until you meet a fence coming in from the right. Follow it to the far corner of the field and go through a gate, then almost immediately right through a gateway. Go diagonally left across the next field. In the far corner, go through

---

Distance – 3¾ miles.

OS Explorer 107 St Austell & Liskeard. GR 139570.

All the paths on this route are fairly easy and clear, and there are few hills to climb. If the tide is particularly high on the stretch around St Winnow, there are directions for avoiding this section, should it be necessary (see point 3).

Starting point The Ship Inn. There is a free public car park alongside the river a few yards from the pub.

How to get there *Lerryn is signposted from the A390 just east of Lostwithiel.*

a gate and down some steps into **Ethy Woods**. The path skirts the top of the wood and then descends. Go through a gap in a fence at the bottom and down to a track; turn right and follow the track across a stream to the ruins of **St Winnow Mill**.

2 Pass the mill and, after a few yards, turn sharp left, following the yellow waymark, and then almost immediately right up some steps to a stile. Follow the field boundary round to the left to a stile; turn right on the other side. At the end cross two stiles in quick succession and bear left after the second. Cross a stile alongside a gate in the middle of the fence ahead and bear left across the next field to another stile alongside a gate in the middle of the left-hand fence. On the other side, follow a track between two fences (do not go into the field on the left). When the track

St Winnow and the River Fowey

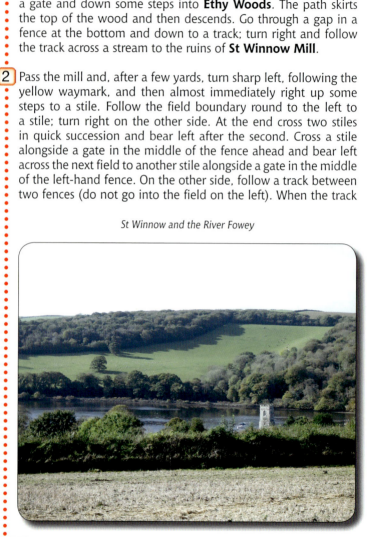

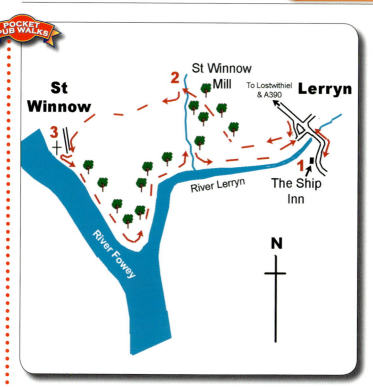

St Winnow
Mill

St
Winnow

To Lostwithiel
& A390

Lerryn

River Lerryn

The Ship
Inn

River Fowey

N

ends, keep right. You now have some lovely views across the countryside ahead and to the left. In the corner of the field, go over two stiles in quick succession on the right and cross the next field. As you go, you get an excellent view across **St Winnow** and the wide expanse of the **River Fowey**. Another stile takes you into a green lane. Go through two gates, and at the lane beyond, turn left.

3 At the bottom of the lane, go into the churchyard. The little church is worth a visit, as it has some particularly good examples of medieval wood carving on some of the pew ends and the

pulpit. Go through the gate on the other side and down to a track; turn left to reach the river. Turn left to follow the shore. At most times there should be plenty of room to walk along the edge of the river. However, if you find that there is no space, then retrace your steps through the churchyard and turn right through a gate. Follow the right-hand boundary through an orchard and you will meet the path higher up.

After a short distance the path leaves the shore and crosses a boardwalk. Go over a stile at the end and keep to the right of a field. Cross another stile and keep right again. A third stile on the right leads you down some steps back into **Ethy Woods**, with the river immediately on your right. The path broadens to a track, and after about ½ mile it leaves the **Fowey** to follow the **Lerryn**. After another ¼ mile you will see a yellow waymark pointing right down some steps. Go down, and follow the path round to the head of the quaintly named **Mendy Pill**, where you cross a stream and continue alongside the **Lerryn**. After a while you join the track again; turn right, and after about 100 yards leave the track to go right again, following the yellow waymark. The path swings left and crosses another stream via a footbridge. Cross a stone stile and go right. Your path joins another, broader, one; go right again. After about ¼ mile the path becomes a track and passes some houses on the edge of **Lerryn**. You come out at a road. If the tide is low, you will find some stepping stones across the river to the car park. If not, turn left and then right after a few yards. At the T-junction turn right and cross the bridge to return to the village.

Places of interest nearby

About 5 miles away, just beyond Lostwithiel, is **Restormel Castle**, an English Heritage property (☎ 01208 872687), and about 3 miles further on you will find the National Trust's **Lanhydrock estate** (☎ 01208 265950).

8 **Perranporth**

The Green Parrot

This relatively easy walk takes you up to the magnificent dune system of Penhale Sands, almost two miles long and stretching a mile inland, and back along the equally lovely Perran Beach – two miles of golden sand. The views from the dunes are superb, and along the way you can visit the sites of the church and oratory of St Piran, a 6th-century saint who is said to have come from Ireland in miraculous circumstances.

THE PUB

The **Green Parrot** is a large, attractive pub, with a comfortable bar divided into cosy alcoves. Upstairs there is another extensive area with tables but also armchairs. Both floors have open fires in winter. A family restaurant and bar is at the

Distance – 4¼ miles.

OS Explorer 104 Redruth & St Agnes. GR 756541.

Apart from one steep climb up steps at the start, the route is quite easy.

Starting point The Green Parrot. There is a car park immediately outside, and if you spend £5 or more in the pub, your parking fee is refunded. Otherwise there is a pay-and-display car park higher up, which is clearly marked.

How to get there Perranporth is on the A3285 between Goonhavern and St Agnes. The Green Parrot is just off Tywarnhayle Square, on the St Agnes road.

side, and a games room at the back. There is also a large and pretty beer garden, with tables on a terraced lawn and a covered patio. The menu ranges from soups and jacket potatoes to steaks, burgers and fish. All the food is locally sourced where possible.

Open from 11 am to 11 pm on Sunday to Thursday and 11 am to 1 am on Friday and Saturday. ☎ 01872 573284

1 Turn left from the car park and go into **Tywarnhayle Square**. Follow the B3285 towards Newquay. After ¼ mile or so the road swings left and, a little later, right. As it swings right again, you will see a public footpath sign on the left pointing up some steps. Turn here and climb the steps to a surfaced track; turn right. Cross another track onto a path, which leads onto a golf course. Cross the golf course, following the row of white stones that mark the public footpath. As you go, you get a good view to the right and back. On the other side of the golf course you come to a road; cross over to a stone stile. Cross a field to another stone stile leading into another road. Turn right and almost immediately left, following the public footpath sign for **Rose**. Follow the path through the gorse and across an open area, which is usually full of rabbits. The next stretch can become rather overgrown, but it is quite passable. It leads you down some steps to a kissing-gate into a field; turn right and follow the right-hand boundary to a gate into a lane.

2 Turn left and follow this lane, flower-fringed in season, to a T-junction. Go straight across to a kissing-gate, following the footpath sign for **St Piran's church and oratory**. This leads you onto **Penhale Sands**, and you immediately get an excellent view of the extensive dune system ahead of you, covered in grass and low bushes. Look out for the posts marked with the acorn waymark and the white stones, both of which indicate the way across the dunes. After ¾ mile you will see a Celtic

A Celtic cross near St Piran's church

45

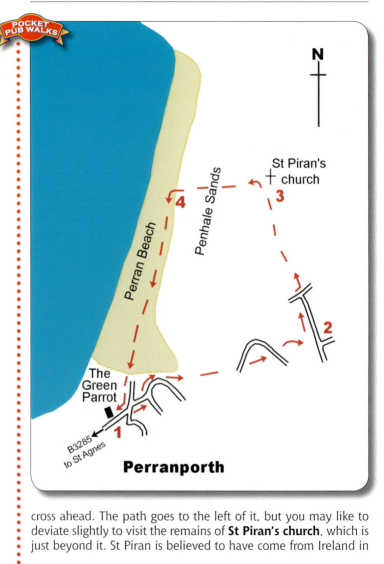

POCKET PUB WALKS

N

St Piran's
✝ church
3

Penhale Sands

4

Perran Beach

2

The
Green
Parrot

1

B3285
to St Agnes

Perranporth

cross ahead. The path goes to the left of it, but you may like to deviate slightly to visit the remains of **St Piran's church**, which is just beyond it. St Piran is believed to have come from Ireland in the 6th century. It is said that he upset the King of Leinster with his miracles, so he was tied to a millstone and thrown into the sea, whereupon he floated across the Irish Sea and came ashore here. He is the patron saint of tinners. The church dates from the 12th century, and the cross from the 11th.

3 Turn left at the church, and rejoin the marked path. It goes down and across a footbridge to the site of **St Piran's oratory**, of which virtually nothing remains visible. On one of the dunes above it stands a concrete cross of modern origin. Continue along the path as it undulates over the dunes and then descends. Soon the sea will become visible, and then the long stretch of **Perran Beach**. Go down to the beach and turn left.

4 Follow the beach for about a mile (you can also follow one of the paths that run along the top of the dunes, but if the tide is relatively low, I prefer the beach). Then, when **Perranporth** comes into view, bear slightly left and go to the right of the **Sunset Bar**. Cross a footbridge and go up some steps to a path which leads to a road. This comes out at **Tywarnhayle Square**, and the **Green Parrot car park** is on the right just beyond.

Places of interest nearby

Two miles east of Perranporth you will find **Miniatura Park**, with miniature scenes from around the world, including Buckingham Palace and the White House, set in 12 acres of gardens (☎ 0870 4584433). About 8 miles away, just off the A3058 south-east of Newquay, is the National Trust's **Trerice**, an Elizabethan manor house (☎ 01637 875404). And about the same distance is **Newquay** itself, which has a large number of attractions, including a zoo and an aquarium (see Walk 6).

9 **Fowey**

The Galleon Inn

Fowey is a delightful old fishing port at the mouth of the river of the same name, with intriguing little lanes stretching up the steep hillside from the quay. This lovely walk follows a route from the top of the town through woods and along farm tracks to a secluded beach, and then back along the coast to the river and the quayside. Along the way you pass some interesting landmarks: an ancient pilgrim route, a ruined castle, and the one-time home of the author Daphne du Maurier. The climb back up to the car park enables you to explore the narrow lanes of the town, lined with traditional houses.

Ideally situated right on the river, the **Galleon** in Fore Street is a relatively modern pub with a lot of atmosphere. Don't be put off by the somewhat unprepossessing façade: inside it is a comfortable, welcoming establishment with some interesting features. It has stone walls and slate floors, with pine beams and comfortable pine furniture. In addition to the main bar, there is a light, airy lounge area, while at the back you will find a lovely, paved, walled garden. The place to be on a sunny day, however, is the riverside patio, with extensive views up and down the river and across to Polruan. The menu ranges from jacket potatoes and paninis to steaks and fish.

Open on Monday to Saturday from 10 am to 12 midnight and on Sunday from 11 am to 11.30 pm. ☎ *01726 833014*

Distance – 4¼ miles.

OS Explorer 107 St Austell & Liskeard. GR 126516 (pub), 122516 (car park).

There are several climbs along this route, and be prepared for one stretch that can become slippery after rain. Perhaps the steepest ascent is the return to the car park from the pub, but this can be avoided if necessary, as there is a minibus service up the hill every fifteen minutes.

Starting point There is no parking in the centre of town, so you will have to park in the main town car park, which is clearly signposted off the main road. This is therefore where the route description starts.

How to get there Follow the A3082 from St Austell or the B3269 from Bodmin and Lostwithiel.

Cornwall

1 Leave the car park at the opposite end from the vehicle entrance, and follow the road. Continue round to the right, and then up to the main road. Turn left. After about ¼ mile you will see a public footpath sign pointing left; ignore it and, after a few yards, follow the next public footpath sign on the left, just before a roundabout. Go through a gate and along a pretty path on the other side. It crosses a bridge and continues down a valley, with banks and hedges on either side. After ½ mile you will come to a road; turn right and walk down to the beach at **Readymoney**. As you pass the beach, you will see a pretty white house on your left; this is where the famous Cornish writer Daphne du Maurier lived briefly during the Second World War.

2 Follow the road to the right, where it ends, and continue along the path on the other side as it climbs into a wood. It is rocky here, and can become slippery when wet. This is the **Saints' Way**, a long-distance route from Padstow to Fowey that connects a number of wells and shrines holy to the Celtic church. At the junction after a short distance, go straight on, following the Celtic cross that is the

St Catherine's Castle

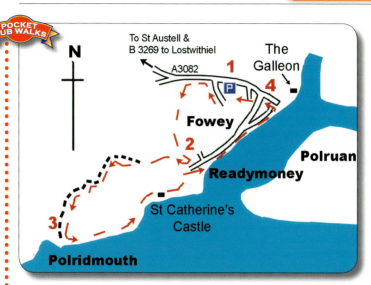

Saints' Way marker. At the next junction, leave the **Saints' Way** and turn left, up some steep steps. This new path continues to climb through the wood until it emerges into a field. You now get a superb view out to sea and along the coast ahead of you. Follow the broad path that curves across the field to a gate. This leads onto a track. You pass a farm on your left (which offers cream teas if you are in need of refreshment at this stage). At the end of the track take the second turning left through a gate (do not take the first left, which leads into a car park). Follow the track (flower-fringed for much of the year) on the other side, and when it swings right follow it. It goes into a field and swings left to follow the hedge. It goes round the edge of the field and then goes left again. At the end it passes through a gate onto another track, which leads down the side of the valley to the coast at **Polridmouth**, with a small lake on your right.

3 Turn left along the **Coast Path**, which climbs some steps. Cross a stile into a field and go through a gate at the end. Follow the

Cornwall

right-hand edge of the next field. Another gate takes you into the next field. At the end, go through another gate and down to the small cove of **Coombe Haven**. There is a steep climb up the other side, and at the end of this field you go through a gate into a wood. At the junction after a few yards, follow the **Coast Path** to the right. You will pass **St Catherine's Castle**, a small artillery fort built by Henry VIII to defend Fowey. It is now in the care of English Heritage, but entry is free. At the next junction, go straight on, rather than taking the path that goes very steeply down to the right. At the next junction, turn right, and at the next one right again. You are now back at **Readymoney**. Take care along this stretch of path as the rocks can be slippery. Follow the road to the left, and continue along it, past the path you came down on. At the junction, carry straight on. At the next junction, when the main road goes left, go straight on again, following the Coast Path sign. You come out at a T-junction in the centre of town; turn right. This lane goes round to the left past the **Aquarium** and you will find yourself on the **Town Quay**, with the **Galleon** straight ahead.

4 Follow the lane back and round to the right past the **Aquarium**. At the junction where you joined this lane, go straight on. After about 100 yards turn left up some steep steps (signposted to the central car park). At the top bear right along a road, which continues to climb to a road. Cross over and climb some more steep steps (again signposted to the central car park). At the top there is a surfaced path with comes out at a road. The car park is straight ahead.

Place of interest nearby

About 4 miles from Fowey, off the B3269, are the **Hidden Valley Gardens**, 4 acres of beautiful gardens set in a lovely valley (☎ 01208 873225).

10 **Looe**

The Harbour Moon

Looe is a very attractive little holiday town divided by the Looe River, with the main centre to the east. Our walk, however, starts in West Looe and follows a ridge above the river of the same name through the lovely Kilminorth Wood, and alongside the ancient earthwork known as the Giant's Hedge. The return leg follows the river downstream, still surrounded by mixed woodland. There is a multitude of bird life on the water – and on the mud at low tide – as well as in the wood.

THE PUB

The **Harbour Moon**, as its name suggests, is a harbourside pub. It has one long, wood-panelled bar with large windows overlooking the river, decorated with nautical knick-knacks. There is a pleasant bistro attached, and tables outside on a terrace, also overlooking the river. As one would expect from

Distance – 3 miles.

OS Explorer 107 St Austell & Liskeard. GR 253535 (pub), 248537 (car park).

There are several fairly easy climbs near the start, but otherwise the going is very easy, with clear paths, some of them surfaced.

Starting point The directions start from the Harbour Moon, but the pub car park is very small, and is for customers only (and it is usually full anyway). The best place to park is in the large car park just off the A387 on the west side of the river. If you are walking direct from the car park, rather than visiting the pub first, then you should start at point 2.

How to get there *The A387 runs straight through Looe from the A38. Follow it across the river to West Looe and you will find the car park signposted to the right. The pub is in Quay Road, the first road on the left after the bridge.*

its location, fresh fish is a speciality, but a range of sandwiches is also served, as well as soup and traditional favourites such as cottage pie. The bistro has a more extensive menu than the bar, but is only open for Sunday lunch and on Thursday, Friday and Saturday evenings out of season (but every day in season).

The pub is open from 11 am to 11 pm on Monday to Saturday and 12 noon to 10.30 pm on Sunday. ☎ *01503 262873*

1 Starting at the pub, follow **Quay Road** back towards the A387. When it climbs to join the main road, bear right and go through a tunnel under the road. Go to the right of the amusement arcade on the other side. Go left beyond the arcade and then right along

a road. When you reach another road, with the car park on the other side, go right, following the public footpath sign. When you reach the river, follow the path to the left. You will come to a boating pool; you can either go straight on along a wall between it and the river, or follow the path to the left – the two join up on the other side. You then skirt a large car park (where you will probably have parked).

2 Soon after the end of the car park, you will come to a junction, with a path sign on the right. Turn left along a surfaced track (signposted as the **Giant's Hedge Walk** to **Watergate**). The track climbs into the beautiful **Kilminorth Wood**. After about 300 yards, you will find a path on the right, leading up some steps (signposted as the **Giant's Hedge Walk** again). The path climbs deeper into the wood, and soon you will find an earth rampart on your left. This is the **Giant's Hedge**, which is believed to have formed the boundary between two Iron Age kingdoms, and stretched all the way to Lerryn, some 8 miles to the north-west. Ignore the various paths you will find leading off to the right; just continue along the main path and you will come to a footbridge. Cross it and follow the path round to the right. Continue to ignore the side paths, and you will eventually come to a junction with a sign pointing right to an alternative return route; you can take this if you wish to shorten the walk, but the main route goes straight on (signposted to **Watergate**). You join a broad track and climb again briefly to a clearing.

3 Here you have another choice. The footpath goes right. It is, however, a steep descent, although made easier by steps. For a gentler but longer route, go straight on (signposted as a bridleway to **Watergate**). This joins a lane, where you should turn right. When you reach the **West Looe River** at **Watergate**, turn right again along a path. If you take the footpath you will make a more direct descent, and end up a short distance from the lane. Turn right (signposted as the **Riverside Walk to Looe**) and go through a gate. This path takes you along the edge of

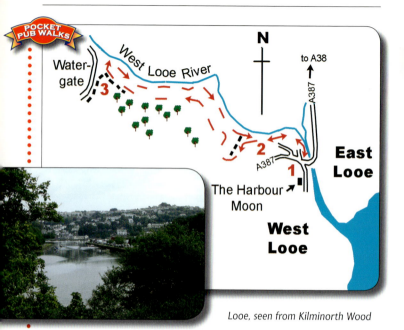

Looe, seen from Kilminorth Wood

the wood, with the sluggish river down on the left. After a little under a mile you will come out onto a surfaced track. Go through a gate at the end and you will be back at the car park. To return to the pub, go to the left, along the riverbank, and at the end turn right. When you come to the road, turn left, and then left and right past the amusement arcade and under the main road to join **Quay Road**.

Place of interest nearby

About 2 miles to the east of Looe is the **Monkey Sanctuary**, a rescue centre for monkeys and home to a colony of woolly monkeys (☎ 01503 262532).

11 St Ives

The Sloop Inn

St Ives is a gem of a town, with little alleys of whitewashed cottages just crying out to be explored. This very varied walk combines a wander through the most delightful parts of the town with country paths and a stunning coastline. The outward leg takes you across farm fields, with good views all around, as well as reminders of Cornwall's mining heritage. The return leg follows the South West Coast Path along the top of the cliffs, with magnificent coastal views, ending with an amble along the beach and harbourside, past the Tate St Ives art gallery, and an exploration of the lanes that stretch up the hillside behind them.

THE PUB

The **Sloop** is a 14th-century inn full of atmosphere and right on the harbourside, with low beams and slate floors. There is a characterful lounge bar with tables and chairs, a more basic

Cornwall

Distance – 5¼ miles

OS Explorer 102 Land's End. GR 516406 (car park), 518407 (pub).

The going is fairly easy but be prepared for some muddy and rough patches along the Coast Path, and a fairly steep but short climb from the pub to the car park.

Starting point The Barnoon car park, in Clodgy View. The car parks in the centre of town are short-stay (and become full very quickly in summer), and this is the closest long-stay car park to both the pub and the route of the walk.

How to get there Follow the A3074 from the A30. Once in St Ives, follow the signs for the car parks. Pass the Trenwith one, which is also signed as a coach park, and continue until you have a choice of turning either left or right for parking; turn left and continue to follow the signs.

public bar furnished with long tables and benches, and with an open fireplace, and a dining area divided into cosy little alcoves. It is decorated with pictures by local artists. There is outside seating both in front, overlooking the sea, and in a small courtyard at the back. The food ranges from sandwiches and baguettes to fresh fish, steaks and home-made specials.

Open from 9 am to 11.30 pm (or if they are busy, 12 midnight) every day. ☎ *01736 796584*

1 The walk description starts from the car park, because that is on the route; if you want to visit the pub first, turn left and go down **Godrevy Terrace**, and then down steps and cobbled lanes to a T-junction. Turn left and left again to reach the **Sloop**.

Turn right from the car park to start the walk and follow **Clodgy**

[f]58

View past a cemetery. You already get a good view over the sea to the right. At the junction at the top of **Clodgy View**, go straight on. You pass a park on the left. At the top, swing left into **Pen-Enys Terrace**, and then right again into **Alexandra Road**. After 100 yards or so, turn right into **Burthallan Lane** (signposted as a no through road). Follow this lane round to the left and out of **St Ives**. You now get a superb view back, past the lighthouse on **Godrevy Island**. Towards the end of the lane, just before it swings left, go left across a stone stile, following the public footpath sign for **Treveal**, **Gurnard's Head** and **Zennor**.

2 A path takes you between high fences and across another stone stile into a field. Keep to the right for a short distance to another stile on the right. Follow the path through the scrub on the other side to a gate. Keep right in the next field for a few yards and then cross another stone stile and keep right in the next field. A succession of fields follows, separated by more stone stiles – keep right all the time. Then, after another

Pen Enys Point

area of scrub, you come to a track; cross over and keep right again in the field on the other side. Go through a gateway and go straight across the next field to another gateway into another field; this time keep left. Cross another stone stile and keep left again; go through a gap in a wall and continue to keep left. Cross yet another stone stile. You now have a good view to your left to **Rosewall Hill** and **Trevalgan Hill**, with the remains of tin mines visible on the former. Two more fields take you to a gate leading into a lane.

3 Cross to a group of holiday homes, and follow the path to the left and the right. At the end of the complex, go to the right to a wooden stile, and keep right in the field beyond. Cross another stile and keep right again. Cross the next field to a gate and keep left, alongside a farm. Go left in the next field to yet another stone stile. Turn immediately right to cross another stone stile and keep left again to a gate. Bear right on the other side, and when you meet a wall, follow it round to another stile. Keep left again and cross two more stone stiles in quick succession. Keep right across five more fields, after which a stone stile takes you into a green lane. Turn right and, at the junction after a few yards, go straight on along a track through a gate. On the other side, leave the track and bear right, aiming for the far corner. Go through a gap in a wall, and keep right along the edge of the next field. You now get another superb view to the right, past a ruined mine engine house and along the coast. Cross a stile, and make your way through the bushes to another stile on your right; cross that to join the **Coast Path**.

4 The path follows the top of the cliff, and you can now enjoy the breathtaking view around the coast ahead of you. You cross a stile and a boardwalk, and go through a kissing-gate along the way, and although the path can become muddy, it is quite clear. After about 1¼ miles you come to a junction in the path. Do not follow the acorn waymark straight on, but turn left, towards the sea. The path swings right and **St Ives** comes into view, with the lovely stretch of **Porthmeor Beach**, ending at **St Ives Head**, ahead of you. You go through a kissing-gate onto a surfaced path, and swing round to the right above the beach.

5 Pass the **Porthmeor short-stay car park** and continue along the road above it. You pass the **Tate St Ives** gallery on your right, and the road swings right and then left. If you want to go straight back to the car park, turn right along a cobbled street (**The Digey**) before the main road goes left. Otherwise continue along the main road, past some pretty houses, until you come to **Fish Street**. Turn down there and you will find the **Sloop** on your right.

To return to the car park from the pub, turn right along the harbourside and then right again into **Fore Street**. After a short distance turn right again into **The Digey** and immediately left into **Virgin Street**. Follow this cobbled alley as it winds between the pretty whitewashed houses and emerges onto a tarred road, **Godrevy Terrace**. Follow that up and you will find the car park on your right.

Places of interest nearby

The walk passes the **Tate St Ives** gallery, an offshoot of Tate Britain devoted to modern and contemporary art, including the St Ives School (☎ 01736 796226). Four miles to the east, near Hayle, you will find **Paradise Park**, a tropical bird garden, which includes an indoor play area (☎ 01736 753365).

12 Sennen Cove

The Old Success Inn

The focus of this lovely walk is the magnificent and well-named Whitesand Bay, whose beach runs for a mile north from Sennen Cove. The first leg takes you across the verdant farmland a little way inland from the bay to the edge of the Nanquidno Downs heathland, with lovely views around the bay. You then return to the coast to join the South West Coast Path, with more excellent views, along the beach to Sennen Cove and beyond. You have a choice of route back to the village: either along the beach or over the dunes.

> **Distance** – 3½ miles.
>
> **OS Explorer** 102 Land's End. GR 354263.
>
> The route follows clear paths, tracks and lanes, most of which are easy to negotiate. There is just one steep climb towards the start.

Starting point The Old Success Inn. The pub has only a small car park, which is reserved for residents. There is, however, a public pay-and-display car park just across the road, another at the harbour at the end of the village, and a third at the top of the hill leading into the village.

How to get there *Turn west off the A30 about a mile from Land's End, following the sign.*

THE PUB

The **Old Success** is ideally placed, opposite a beautiful beach, and with magnificent sea views. It is a 17th-century establishment, with a long beamed and timbered bar decorated with various reminders of the area's maritime heritage, especially the lifeboats. There is also a separate restaurant, and a terraced garden. The bar menu ranges from sandwiches, pasties and jacket potatoes to steak and kidney pie and local fish.

Open from 11 am to 11 pm on Monday to Saturday and from 11.30 am to 10.30 pm on Sunday. ☎ *01736 871232*

1 Turn right on leaving the pub and go into the public car park. Towards the end, take the **Coast Path** up into the dunes. You immediately get a superb view along the length of **Whitesand Bay**. At the first path junction, go straight on and, at the second, straight on again, following the acorn **Coast Path** waymark. At the third junction, just before a wooden house, leave the

Cornwall

Coast Path to take the path on the right, which climbs up the dunes and round a stone wall. It is a steep climb, but if you pause for breath along the way, you will get another excellent view back along the beach to **Sennen Cove** and beyond. At the top,

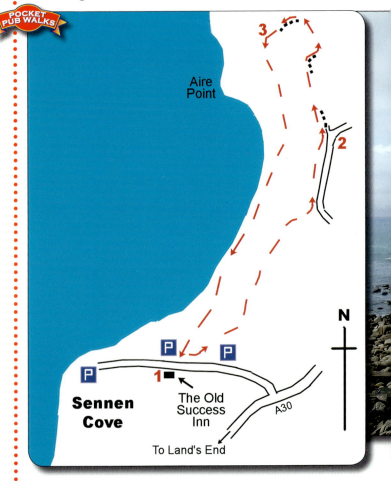

when you come to a rocky outcrop, the path turns right. At the junction after a few yards, go left. You will come to a broad path between walls; go left. When this path joins a track go right, and at the surfaced lane after a short distance, left.

Aire Point

Cornwall

2 When the lane swings right to some houses, go straight on through a gateway onto a track. Go through another gateway and follow the track on the other side. At the end of the field turn right to follow the fence round. About halfway along, turn left across a stile, following the yellow waymark. Go straight across the next field to another stile. You can now see the heathland of **Nanquidno Downs** across the valley to your right. Cross the next field to another stile in the far right-hand corner. This leads onto a track; turn left. Go through a farmyard and, at the end, you will be faced by two gates; take the right-hand one and follow the track on the other side, which runs between two walls, and soon narrows to a path.

3 Go through a gate at the end and bear left to follow the path on the other side. At the bottom of the field it swings left to follow the cliff. You now get a lovely view along **Whitesand Bay**. The path descends gently at first and then quite steeply to join the **Coast Path** above a rock field, with **Aire Point** to the right. Turn left and follow the path above the rocks. When they give way to sand, you can either continue along the **Coast Path** or go down and follow the beach back to **Sennen Cove**. If you take the beach route, go up along a slipway and through the car park to return to the pub.

Place of interest nearby

About 1½ miles away is **Land's End**, the westernmost point in England, where there is a theme park with a wide range of activities and attractions (☎ 0871 7200044).

13 Constantine

The Trengilly Wartha Inn

Woods and water are the main features of this delightful ramble. A quiet lane takes you from the pub, which lies a short distance outside Constantine itself, to join a track through a cool, lush wood. You then follow the pretty Ponjeravah stream up through mixed woodland to the top of the valley, and then back down to the village. Farm paths with excellent views bring you back to the Trengilly Wartha.

Cornwall

Distance – 2¾ miles.

OS Explorer 103 The Lizard. GR 731282.

Apart from one steep climb at the start, this is an easy route along clear paths, lanes and tracks.

Starting point The Trengilly Wartha Inn. Customers may leave their cars in the inn car park while they walk, but please ask first. If you are not planning to visit the pub, you can park in the free car park in Constantine, and start the walk at point 4.

How to get there *Constantine can be reached from the A39 Truro to Falmouth road via Mabe or the A394 from Helston to Falmouth, or from the A3083 between Helston and the Lizard via Gweek. The Trengilly Wartha Inn is about a mile from the village, a short distance off the Gweek road, from which it is clearly signposted.*

THE PUB The pretty **Trengilly Wartha Inn** is set in an idyllic position in a lovely valley, with gardens stretching down to a lake and stream (although food and drink are not allowed in the gardens). The public accommodation consists of a long bar furnished with settles and tables, with dark beams decorated with beer mats, a large conservatory with games for children, and a light, airy bistro with an open fireplace. There is also a separate restaurant. Outside, there is a patio with tables and seats. The menu includes light meals such as salads, soup and burgers, as well as more substantial fare such as lasagne and meat and fish dishes.

Open in summer from 11 am to 3 pm and 6 pm to 12 midnight. In winter, the evening opening is half an hour later.
☎ *01326 340332*

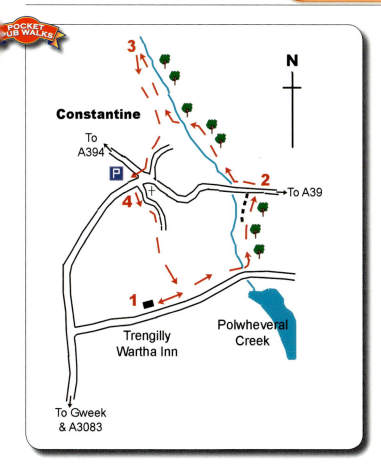

POCKET PUB WALKS

3

Constantine

To
A394

P

4

2

→To A39

N

1

Trengilly
Wartha Inn

Polwheveral
Creek

To Gweek
& A3083

1 Follow the pub's drive to the lane and turn left. Cross a stream, and follow the lane as it climbs steeply out of the valley. When it reaches the top it descends just as steeply into another valley. Cross another stream, the **Ponjeravah**, and when the lane turns right, go left up a track, following the public footpath sign. The track becomes a pretty path running through a wood, with the

A woodland track near Constantine

stream cascading over the rocks on the left. After a short distance it joins a track; turn left. The track then emerges onto a lane; turn left again.

2 After a few yards, when you come to the **Constantine village sign**, turn right and then immediately left, following the public

bridleway sign. Follow the broad track as it winds through the lovely wood, still with the stream on your left. After almost ½ mile, when the track goes right to a farm, turn left to cross a footbridge and continue upstream on the other side.

3 After ¼ mile you will see a path coming in from the left; turn sharp left along it. (If you find yourself crossing the stream again, you will have gone too far, and should retrace your steps for a few yards.) This path takes you up and along the edge of the wood, with an old wall on your right and the stream occasionally visible below you on the left. You cross a stone stile and eventually leave the wood and emerge at a track. Cross it and follow the path on the other side, between a wall on the left and a fence on the right. Go down some steps and onto a road, and turn right. At the T-junction turn right and after a few yards left (signposted to **Gweek**, **Helston** and the **Lizard**).

4 After 50 yards, turn left past the church, following the sign for the **Health Centre**, also marked as a public bridleway. When the road ends, follow the track ahead. You now get a lovely view in front of you over the rolling farmland. At the end of the track, cross a stone stile. Cross a track to a wooden stile and bear right across the field beyond to a stone stile. Go straight across the next field to another stile, leading into a lane; turn right and follow the lane down the hill and across the stream to the **Trengilly Wartha Inn** up its drive on the right.

Places of interest nearby

At Gweek, about 2½ miles away, is the **National Seal Sanctuary** (☎ 01326 221361). About 3 miles in the other direction (south-east) is Mawnan Smith, which is home to two valley gardens: **Trebah** (☎ 01326 252200) and the National Trust's **Glendurgan** (☎ 01326 862090).

14 **Treen**

The Logan Rock Inn

This is a particularly delightful route, combining farm paths, tracks and lanes with outstanding coastal and countryside views. The first leg crosses farm fields, with the views starting almost immediately. You then head down to skirt the village of Porthcurno, famous for the magnificent open-air Minack Theatre, built into the cliff to the south, and join the South West Coast Path, where you can enjoy more views, this time along the coast. After you have visited the pretty hamlet of Penberth, a tree-fringed lane brings you back to Treen.

THE PUB

The **Logan Rock** is a 400-year-old granite inn with a warm atmosphere. It has a low-beamed bar with an open fireplace, a family room with games, and a little snug decorated with cricket artefacts. There are also two patios, one at the back and the other in the front. The food is excellent, and ranges from

Distance – 3¾ miles.

OS Explorer 102 Land's End. GR 394231.

The route is generally fairly easy, following farm paths and tracks. There is one climb along a lane towards the end, but otherwise it is relatively flat.

Starting point The Logan Rock Inn. Customers who are eating at the pub may leave their cars in the pub car park while walking, provided they ask first. Otherwise there is a pay-and-display car park at the end of the village.

How to get there *The village is just off the B3315 between St Buryan and Land's End, and is signposted.*

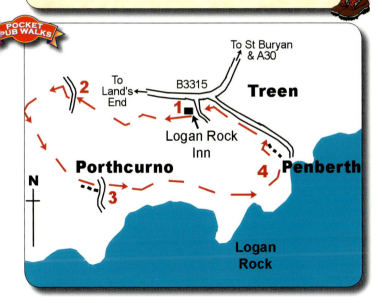

basket meals and jacket potatoes to a wide variety of main courses, including local fish.

Open from 10.30 am to 11 pm every day in summer and from 10.30 am to 2.30 pm and 5 pm to 11 pm in winter.
☎ *01736 810495*

1 Turn right as you leave the pub, and after a short distance, as the road turns left, go right along a track, following the public footpath sign. At the end, go through a gate and keep to the left of the field on the other side. You now get an excellent view up the valley to your right. Go through a gateway at the end of the field, and keep to the left again to another gateway. Go straight across the next field to another gate and keep to the right beyond that. Cross a stone stile and bear left to reach another one. Follow the path across the next field towards some farm buildings. Go through a gateway at the end and turn left. Cross a stile alongside a gate and turn right to follow the right-hand boundary. Go through a gate and bear left along a path that goes diagonally across the next field. You meet up with a wall on your left; follow it and turn right at the end to follow the field boundary round to a stile. You now have another lovely view of the lush farmland ahead of you. Keep to the right of the next field to a gateway leading into a lane.

2 Turn right and, after 100 yards, left across a stile, following the public footpath sign. Go straight across the field on the other side. Cross another stile and go straight across the next field. In the next field, aim for the far right-hand corner. Go through a gate and bear left to a stile in the middle of the left-hand hedge. On the other side, do not go straight on, following the yellow waymark, but bear left along another path to a gate. On the other side, go straight on to a stone stile in the wall ahead. Walk straight across the next field to two gates. Go through the left-hand one, and keep to the right of the field on the other side. At the end, go through a kissing-gate and past some houses. Continue left and right through the complex and follow the surfaced track on the other side. When it emerges onto a lane, turn left.

3 Follow the lane down a hill and at the bottom turn right along a drive, following the public bridleway sign. At the end of the drive, bear left to follow the path. When you come to a track, turn left and almost immediately right, following the blue bridleway waymark. The path climbs between high bushes; at the double junction at the top go straight on, following the acorn **Coast Path** waymark. You now get a superb view to the right, with the **Logan**

The coast near Treen

Rock half-right, and the **Minack Theatre** on the cliff behind you. Continue for about a mile.

4 The path descends steeply to the pretty fishing hamlet of **Penberth**. Turn left along a track at the bottom and, after a few yards, turn right to cross a footbridge. Turn left on the other side, along a delightful tree-fringed lane, with the stream running down alongside. It climbs steadily for about ½ mile to the main road; turn left, and after a few yards left again (signposted to the **Logan Rock** and **Treen**). The pub is on the right after a few yards.

Places of interest nearby

The **Minack Theatre** (see walk description) is only 1½ miles away (☎ 01736 810181). **Land's End**, the westernmost point in England, where there is a theme park with a wide range of activities and attractions is 3 miles away. (☎ 0871 7200044).

15 Mullion

The Old Inn

The views on this route will take your breath away – the panorama round Mounts Bay to Land's End accompanies you for much of the walk and there are also excellent views across the farms and woods inland. There is a cost, in the form of some steep climbs, but believe me, they are worth it. Clear paths and tracks take you from Mullion to Polurrian Cove, where you join the South West Coast Path for the cliff-top stretch to Mullion Cove and Mullion Cliff beyond. You then turn inland and follow farm paths back to Mullion.

THE PUB

This interesting granite 16th-century pub is easy to get lost in! As well as the main bar the **Old Inn** has no fewer than four lounges and seating areas, some leading into each other. All the rooms have low, black beams and there is a wood-burning stove in the bar and an open fireplace in one of the lounges. Another lounge has what was an enormous hearth, now an alcove containing seating. There are also tables outside. The menu includes sandwiches, salads and soup, as well as main courses that range from local fish to steaks.

Open from 11 am to 11 pm during the week and from 11 am to 12 midnight at weekends. ☎ *01326 240240*

1 Turn right as you leave the **Old Inn** and, after about 100 yards, take the surfaced public footpath on the right, between houses on the left and a playground on the right. It comes out at a road; go straight on. At the T-junction go straight on again, along another surfaced path. At the end go down some steps to a lane

Distance – 4 miles.

OS Explorer 103 The Lizard. GR 678192.

The paths are clear, but be prepared for some steep climbs along the Coast Path.

Starting point The Old Inn. The pub does not have a car park, but there is a free public car park across the road.

How to get there *Take the B3296 west off the A3083 between Helston and the Lizard. When you reach Mullion, continue along the B3296 towards Poldhu and you will find the pub a few yards up the road on your left and the car park on your right.*

Cornwall

and go straight on again. The lane deteriorates to a track; when that turns right along a private road, bear left, following the blue bridleway waymark. This attractive path between high hedges leads you down to the sea, where you join the **Coast Path** just above the pretty beach at **Polurrian Cove**, with **Mullion Island** to the left.

2 Turn left and cross a small bridge, then climb some steep steps up the hillside on the other side. At the top of the steps the path goes under a footbridge, and continues to climb more gently. At the top you get a breathtaking view all around **Mounts Bay** to

Mullion Cove and Mullion Island

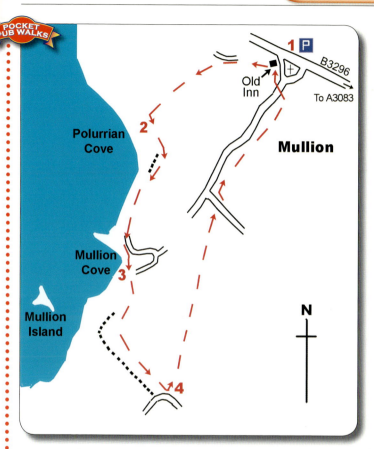

POCKET
PUB WALKS

1 P

B3296

Old
Inn

To A3083

Polurrian
Cove

2

Mullion

Mullion
Cove

3

Mullion
Island

N

4

Land's End. Turn right along a track, following the **Coast Path** sign for **Mullion Cove**. When the track swings left to a house, go straight on along a path, still with the view around the bay on your right. The path eventually comes out at a road; turn right and follow it past the **Mullion Cove Hotel**. At the end of the car park opposite the hotel, go right, following the acorn **Coast Path** waymark. This path takes you steeply down to **Mullion Cove**.

Cornwall

3 Cross the slipway, climb some steps on the other side and turn left, following the **Coast Path** sign. After a few yards turn sharp right, again following the **Coast Path** sign. The path climbs steeply, but at the top you are rewarded with another view around **Mounts Bay**. You cross a footbridge over a small gully, and about 100 yards beyond it, at a fence, the path forks; go right, following the main track, which leads round the coast. It joins another track; turn left. This track emerges onto a surfaced lane; just before it does so, turn left alongside a wall, following the public footpath sign.

4 Cross a stile and keep to the right of the field on the other side. Cross another stile and keep to the right again. You now have a 180° panorama ahead of you, from **Mounts Bay** on the left across to the rolling countryside on the right. There is a wayside cross in the corner of the field on your right. Go over a third stile and keep to the right again; a fourth stile takes you onto a path between high bushes, with wild flowers galore alongside in season. You cross an open area and go through a gap in a hedge into another field; keep right. At the end cross a track and then follow the path on the other side between high bushes again. Yet another stile takes you into yet another field; keep to the right as before, and to the right of the field beyond, and the one beyond that. A final stile takes you onto a lane; turn left and follow it up a hill to a road; turn right and follow the road into **Mullion**. In the centre of the village, bear left and pass the church to reach the **Old Inn**.

Places of interest nearby

Flambards theme park is about 7 miles from Mullion, near Helston (☎ 01326 573404). At Gweek, about the same distance away north-east, is the **National Seal Sanctuary** (☎ 01326 221361).